BEGINNER**JAZZ** **PIANO**SOLOING

Discover Jazz Piano Soloing for Beginners & Quickly Learn to Improvise

NATHAN**HAYWARD**

FUNDAMENTAL**CHANGES**

Beginner Jazz Piano Soloing

Discover Jazz Piano Soloing for Beginners & Quickly Learn to Improvise

ISBN: 978-1-78933-244-5

Published by **www.fundamental-changes.com**

www.fundamental-changes.com

Cover Image Copyright: Shutterstock, Nomad_Soul

Special thanks

Thanks to my friend, Chris Evans, who helped me with the recording and played the ride cymbal so beautifully. Also, to my lovely wife, Rachel, for giving me the space to do the work and for your encouragement. *–Nathan*

Contents

Introduction

Jazz is a language. It has its own musical vocabulary that, when spoken well, is one of the most distinctive, beautiful and dynamic means of creative musical expression. Just as you can't put on a French accent and say that you speak French, you can't play something *jazzy* and call it "jazz". There's much more to learning a language than that. We need to know the words, the phrases, and the subtle nuances that make up the language.

When I talk about using the language of jazz, I'm referring to our ability to *improvise* – to speak it fluently; to be able to invent melodic phrases to solo over chords. Some find the thought of improvisation intimidating, especially if they learned piano in a classical way. If this is you, don't forget that you improvise every single day when you speak!

Every day we talk to people without any forethought as to what we're going to say. We respond to what others are saying, and often fall back on stock words or phrases, but essentially, we're improvising. The secret is to know the language well.

In order to feel comfortable with the jazz language we must listen to it. When we were children, we learned to talk by listening, watching and copying others. It's the same for music. We know that one of the best ways to learn a new language is to live where it is spoken and immerse ourselves in it. Jazz has always been an aural tradition, so immerse yourself in the sounds of the great jazz artists.

We must also study it and learn the scales (alphabet), motifs (words) and licks (sentences) to know what to say, and how to respond to what is happening in the musical conversation.

I hope this book will help you on your way to learning this phenomenal musical language and that it keeps inspiring you as you improve.

What You'll Learn from This Book

In this book we're going to explore language built around the major and minor pentatonic and blues scales, then use them to create some authentic jazz sounds. To begin with, we'll focus on getting the ideas and melodies happening in the right hand before learning what the left hand should be doing in chapters six and seven. When you've completed them, you'll be able to return to the earlier examples in the book and add the chords to make them into complete musical pieces.

You'll learn to understand and hear each concept thoroughly by learning *licks,* which will mostly be two-bar musical phrases. Together we'll be listening to, memorising and composing licks, so that you begin to grow a basic vocabulary for soloing. When you have a collection of ideas you can begin to connect them together in sentences to form solos.

Next, you'll learn to mix and match your licks to invent spontaneous phrases built on similar rhythms and melodic patterns. Remember that when a jazz musician is improvising, they're not picking notes out of thin air but drawing on a vast storehouse of melodic and rhythmic ideas. These ideas can be brought together, combined and shaped into something fresh and new in the moment. This is the basis of all jazz soloing.

As we explore the role of the left hand, we'll look at some basic, yet important chord voicings you'll use to play songs and underpin your solos. These will build into the chord progressions you need to know, before you learn to solo over *chord changes* with arpeggio-based ideas.

These skills are the essence of jazz playing, but don't be worried if they sound a little intimidating. We'll go step-by-step and work through each idea before gradually adding more detailed layers so that you're never overwhelmed.

By the end of this book, you'll have built up a musical vocabulary that will help you to solo convincingly over simple jazz chord sequences, and you'll be beginning to explore your own licks and ideas in original solos.

Get the Audio

The audio files for this book are available to download for free from **www.fundamental-changes.com.** The link is in the top right-hand corner. Click on the "Guitar" link then simply select this book title from the drop-down menu and follow the instructions to get the audio.

We recommend that you download the files directly to your computer, not to your tablet, and extract them there before adding them to your media library. You can then put them onto your tablet, iPod or burn them to CD. On the download page there are instructions and we also provide technical support via the contact form.

For over 350 free guitar lessons with videos check out:

www.fundamental-changes.com

Join our free Facebook Community of Cool Musicians

www.facebook.com/groups/fundamentalguitar

Tag us for a share on Instagram: **FundamentalChanges**

Chapter One – The Major Pentatonic Scale

With every musical idea, the first question we should always ask ourselves is *how does it sound?* Every scale, chord or lick we learn has its own character that needs to be appreciated. Even if we understand what should work in theory, we won't be able to use a concept convincingly until we instinctively know its *flavour*. Always listen carefully to the sounds you're making as you work through each example.

In the first five chapters of this book, we're going to work only with the right hand to develop your melodic vocabulary without any distractions. We'll begin by learning the major pentatonic scale. Pentatonic scales are used extensively in jazz soloing and are an accessible way for the prospective jazz pianist to quickly create a jazz sound. In fact, this scale will work over most major key chord sequences and it provides a good framework if you want something simple and tasteful to play.

The major pentatonic is a simple scale that consists of just five notes. In C Major it contains the notes C, D, E, G and A. This is how it sounds:

Example 1a

Take some time to absorb the sound of this scale. Play up and down the scale notes. Experiment by playing different combinations of the notes while holding down a C Major chord or C bass note.

One of the best ways to internalise a jazz lick or scale is to sing it. It doesn't matter whether you're a proficient singer or not – this is just for practice. Try singing the scale at the same time as playing it to help feel its sound and character.

Notice that C Major Pentatonic has a "stable" sound and doesn't contain any half step intervals. Try playing two-, three- or four-note combinations at random and you'll hear that nothing sounds particularly discordant. I describe the major pentatonic sound as "fresh plain bread" – a simple pleasure.

Major Pentatonic licks

In most chapters, I will be asking you to learn *five* licks. Your task is to memorise them, just as you would memorise stock phrases when learning a spoken language. This is essential!

These five short licks use the notes of the C Major Pentatonic scale and will form the first parts of your jazz language. The better you learn them, the more natural and fluent your speech (soloing) will be.

Listen to the licks and learn them as much by ear as from the notation. Try to sing them too. When you're comfortable with each phrase, play along with me on the audio recordings. In each recording I play the lick eight times to help you absorb it through repetition.

In this first lick, we move back and forth between just two notes of the C Major Pentatonic scale, C and A. The important thing is to get the *rhythm* and *feel* of the line spot on. Practice it until you can play it perfectly in sync with the recording.

Example 1b

Listen to the way the next lick is played on the recording. Notice how the notes are not smooth and joined up. The 1/4 notes are slightly detached from the others, which creates a light, springy sound. *How* you play notes is important and it's good to develop the skill of accurately mimicking what you hear, so try to get it sounding exactly like the recording.

Example 1c

Example 1d is a tiny "cell" of an idea that could be part of a longer melodic line. Short ideas like this can go a long way, simply by moving them around within a bar of music. When you've memorised it, try playing it starting on the first beat of the bar. Now try beginning the idea on beats two, three or four. How does it sound? The more flexible you can be, the more use you'll get from it.

Example 1d

You'll need to put your hand in a different position for Example 1e as it uses the notes C and E an octave higher than we've played so far. When you create your own licks, remember that they don't all have to be in the same octave or hand position. Use the scale to its full potential.

Example 1e

The last of our five major pentatonic licks uses all of the notes of the scale and ducks under the octave to reach for the A note below middle C. However, don't fall into the trap of thinking that more notes are better. Often, the opposite is true, and most of the time *using fewer notes is better!*

Example 1f

Compose your own licks

You may think that *composing* a lick (i.e. deliberately planning it out) is not the same as *improvising,* but when you compose a lick you are simply slowing down the process of improvisation and giving yourself a chance to think more reflectively about how to use the scale. The following exercises will help you to get creative with the major pentatonic scale.

Use this page to compose four of your own major pentatonic licks using what you've learned so far.

First, keep them *simple.* Remember that using fewer notes often leads to a better result. It also makes the lick easier to play!

Second, keep them *short.* The shorter the lick, the more memorable it will be. Later, you'll be able to string these ideas together to create longer musical lines. The licks you write here are also part of your jazz vocabulary, so keep them short and sweet.

Third, think of simple, *strong rhythms.* We already know the notes sound good, so use a catchy rhythm to build a strong line.

Below are four, two-bar treble clef staves in 4/4. I want you to write your licks in 4/4 for now, so that you can play them with the backing track. Most licks can be adapted easily for other time signatures later.

When you have composed a lick, play it multiple times with the provided backing track. Try beginning your lines on different beats of the bar to see how they feel.

Lick 1

Lick 2

Lick 3

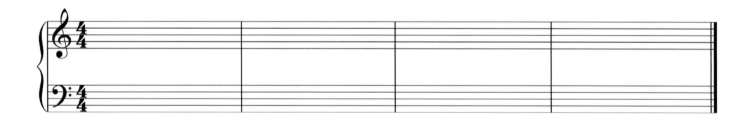

Lick 4

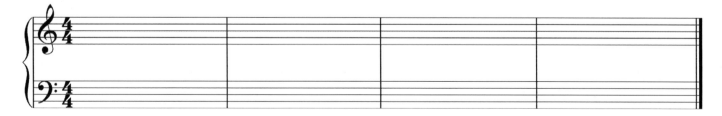

Learn a tune

To finish this chapter, I want you to learn a simple tune I've written that combines the major pentatonic language you've learnt into actual music. It's written in the *swing* style of the 1930-40s. Seek out the piano playing of Count Basie and Duke Ellington to hear the feel we're aiming for. Remember, we're not adding any left-hand notes at this stage, but I've included the chord symbols for when you revisit this tune later.

Before you play anything, listen to the audio recording. The melody section is played as written, then there's a solo using only the notes of the major pentatonic scale. Hear how effectively the major pentatonic can be used in a solo. After the solo, the melody returns to finish the piece.

Example 1g

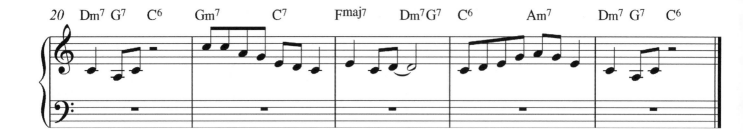

Once you have learned the melody above, play along to the Chapter One backing track and try adding your own solo using my licks and the ones you've written yourself. Mix and match them to create different ideas every time you come to the solo part. When you get more confident, see if you can invent some spontaneous ideas too.

In the next chapter, we're going to add a different flavour to our plain bread scale to make things sound more interesting.

Chapter Two – The Blues Scale

The blues scale has a distinct, recognisable flavour that's quite unlike the major pentatonic scale we've just studied. As you might expect, it is used extensively in Blues and Jazz. For the jazz pianist it is an important flavour to have on hand to use at any given moment – in fact, every jazz musician I know has a whole catalogue of blues licks at their disposal.

The blues scale is versatile and doesn't have to be played on any specific chord. Rather, it can assert its strong character over whole chord progressions and normally works brilliantly as long as you are playing in the correct key.

The notes of the C Blues scale are C, Eb, F, Gb/F#, G and Bb.

Notice the Gb/F# note. Some musicians are taught the C Blues scale with the fifth note as a Gb, so that it looks like this:

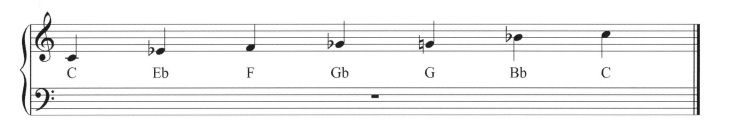

Jazz pianists, however, normally understand that note as a Gb when played as part of a *descending* lick, but an F# when played as part of an *ascending* lick. In this book we use it in the latter context, notating a Gb when descending and an F# when ascending. This rule will occasionally also apply to an Eb note, which will be notated D# when ascending to an E natural.

Play the scale now, listen carefully to how it sounds, then memorise it.

Example 2a

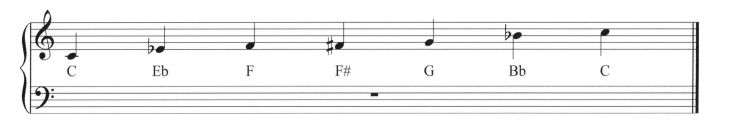

Take some time to absorb the sound of this scale. You can play up and down the scale notes or experiment by playing different combinations of notes. Remember to sing along as you play, as this helps to internalise the sounds. Play around with the scale over a C bass note and you'll quickly feel it's unique flavour.

Let's take a moment to stop and think about the character of each note.

C – The tonic or "home" note. If you want to close down a passage of music, end on the tonic note. When you play this note it sounds like you've arrived home. It is a safe note that you can use often.

Eb – the first bluesy note. Eb is the third note in the C *Minor* scale, yet in blues we play it frequently over C *Major* chords to create the minor against major tension which gives the blues its flavour. You can mix and match this note with the "major sounding" E natural. Some people include the E natural in their version of the blues scale, so they can play around with the major/minor tonality.

F – a good passing note or jumping off note to start your ideas, but not so good for ending your phrases.

F# – the most bluesy of blue notes and the most far out sounding note of the scale. This note helps create the delightful three-note chromatic run of F, F#, to G in the centre of the blues scale. It is also a great note to start a blues lick on. Most often you'll use it *en route* to another note, and ending a lick on this note is not always advisable.

G – another good "safe" note to play, it will work almost any place in your solo. It is a particularly good note on which to end an "open phrase" (a phrase that sounds like it should be followed by another. Read on to find out more about open and closed phrases).

Bb – another minor against major tension note. In functional harmony, the 7th note of the major scale is important and named the *leading note* because it leads strongly back to the root. The 7th note in the C Major scale is a B natural, but the blues scale blunts its leading note function by flattening it to create a completely different sound that's a world away from classical harmony.

Blues scale licks

Here are five licks that use the C Blues scale. Remember, it's important to learn these licks well to build a musical vocabulary that you have instant access to. Think of it as learning some lines for a play, or some jokes for a comedy night.

Our first blues scale lick is simple. Listen to how it is played on the recording. The second note (C) is *ghosted* (in other words, hardly audible). Ghost notes are notes that you can hardly hear but they add a different feel to a line. Good *feel* is something that we can develop by lots of listening to, and mimicking of, the great jazz players. Eventually you'll start to feel where best to use ghost notes in your solos.

Example 2b

Example 2c starts on the bluesy note of F#. Immediately, the dissonance of this note is resolved by moving up to G, only to dip down again and resolve in the same way. This principle of tension and resolution is important in all kinds of music and is often at play in the blues. Pushing out to the more bluesy notes and then resolving them (or sometimes delaying the resolution to create additional tension) is integral to playing good blues.

We also see some triplets in this lick that create some rhythmic interest by breaking up the monotony of an all 1/8th note line.

Example 2c

Our next lick starts on Bb and jumps down to Gb to create quite a far-out sound which is resolved immediately by the familiar blues phrase of F, Eb and C. The lick ends on the note of G to create an *open phrase*. An open phrase is one that sounds like it's leading on to another.

Try ending the lick on the note C instead of G, and notice that it now sounds more final – like the answer to a question. Now play the lick twice, the first-time ending on G (as written) and the second time ending on C. You may notice that the first time sounds like a question and the second time sounds like the answer.

When we ask a question, the intonation of our voice often goes up at the end, expecting a response, and when we give the answer the intonation of our voice often goes down. The same thing is happening musically.

Example 2d

I've written Example 2e out twice to introduce you to a cool little trick. As mentioned earlier, C is a *safe* note play, being the tonic or home note. It is *so safe* that you can use it in combination with any other note of the blues scale and it will sound great. Here, I've used it to give emphasis to the F# notes and I generally use the C above my chosen melody, but you can use it below too. Experiment with this trick on the other licks.

This strategy can be used to great effect to intensify your solo. You may want to start a blues solo with more sparse, single-note ideas, but as you progress through your solo, you'll want to lift it to a new level of excitement.

Example 2e

Our final blues scale lick starts with the trick we've just learned. The C – Gb combination at the beginning of this lick is particularly pleasing and common in blues soloing, so make it a regular part of your playing. At the end of the first bar there is a little *grace note,* an F# sliding up to a G. A grace note mimics the slide that can be achieved by a voice or a saxophone.

Example 2f

Compose your own licks

Now it's time for you to get creative again and compose your own blues scale licks. Don't forget to revisit the previous licks you have written.

Use the rhythms and shapes of my lines to inspire your own licks. Play similar rhythms with different notes, or different rhythms with the same notes. Licks can be short or long, fast or slow, predictable or surprising. When you have composed a lick, play it multiple times with the provided backing track and sing it too.

Lick 1

Lick 2

Lick 3

Lick 4

To end this chapter, I want you to learn another simple tune. This one is written in the style of an Oscar Peterson blues. If you've not heard his playing before, go online to search him out. A good place to start is his album *Night Train*.

There's still no left hand at this stage, but I've included the chord symbols for when you revisit this tune later on.

Listen to the audio recording of this piece. The melody section is played as written, then there's a solo using only the notes of the C Blues scale. After the solo, the melody returns to finish the piece.

Example 2g

Once you have learned the melody above, play along with the Chapter Two backing track in your audio download. Mix and match the licks you've learned in this chapter to create different ideas every time you come to the solo part. Enjoy playing along and do it as much as possible. When you get more confident, see if you can invent some spontaneous ideas too.

In the next chapter, we're going to start mixing the two different flavours we've learned to make your solo sound even more interesting.

Chapter Three – Mixing the Scales

In this chapter we're going to combine the jazz piano knowledge and tools we've gained so far to make a more melodically interesting solo. The two scales we've explored have different characters: C Major Pentatonic is plain and simple, while the blues scale has a more distinctive flavour. These two ingredients combine beautifully and there's a world of pleasure to be found in blending them – kind of like making a sandwich with whatever filling you choose!

In the previous chapter I made reference to the music of Oscar Peterson. Continue to immerse yourself in his music, because this combination of scales forms a large part of his musical vocabulary.

A couple of classic note combinations

First, there are two pentatonic/blues scale note combinations I want you to explore.

The first is mentioned in the previous chapter – to play the Eb of the blues scale against the E natural of the major pentatonic scale. It results in the classic blues major/minor ambiguity which is so integral to the style.

The second combination brings the Eb of the blues scale with the A natural of the major pentatonic. This is a great combination which can be used in single note melodic phrases or played together at the same time.

Look out for these combinations in the following five licks.

Blues/major pentatonic licks

In our first lick, we'll make use of the Eb/A natural combination. I've deliberately kept this line short so you can add it as a little cell within larger phrases. Learn it perfectly and internalise the sound that the A and Eb create. Learn it so well that you can play it with your eyes shut, then you'll be able to couple it with other ideas naturally, without having to stop and think.

Example 3a

For our second lick, we're going to develop the notes from the first. This is a good example of how you can create a longer solo by taking a short idea and kicking it around. Here, I've simply chosen to play the idea three times. Repeating the phrase continuously, with no rest, displaces it, so that it begins on different beats of the bar. The first repetition lands on beat 1, the second repetition on beat 4, and the third repetition on beat 3 of the next bar.

To finish the lick, I *invert* the idea and use triplets to create a little flourish at the end. Rhythmic displacement and inversion are two great strategies you can use to develop your own musical ideas.

Example 3b

Next, we have some tasty two-note combinations played as momentary chords in the right hand. We start with the A and Eb combination, played together as a two-note chord. In the second bar we use the bluesy combination of C and Gb as a momentary dissonant chord that immediately resolves to the note F.

We end the lick with an implied F Major chord (F and A played together) followed by a C Major chord (E and G combined).

Example 3c

Our next idea is a lot of fun. We're going to use the same chord idea again on beats 2 and 3 of bars one and two, but this time as part of a figure played in descending 3rds. We approach the chords from the notes above, G and Bb in bar one, and Gb and Bb in bar two to create a slightly more "out there" variation. This use of fleeting chords in the right hand is quite stylistic and works well as long as you bring things home by resolving them.

Example 3d

Our final lick is a single note line. After the initial D# we ascend up to C using the notes of the major pentatonic scale. Then we descend using the blues scale to create the typical balance of colours that makes the major pentatonic/blues scale combination so pleasing.

Example 3e

Compose your own licks

Now it's time for you to get creative again and compose your own combination licks.

As always, write and play these over the backing track and use the rhythms and shapes of the previous ideas to help you compose your own phrases.

Lick 1

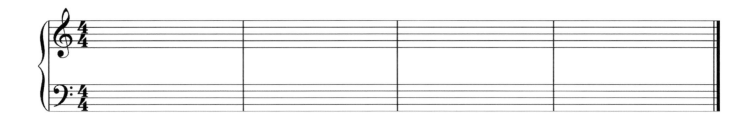

Lick 2

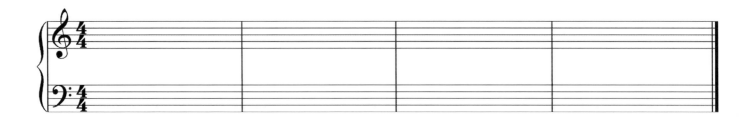

Lick 3

Lick 4

To end this chapter, we've another simple tune to learn, written in the style of Oscar Peterson again. We're still not adding any left-hand notes at this stage, but I've included the chord symbols for when you revisit this tune later on.

The melody section is played as written, then there's a solo using only the notes of the C Major Pentatonic and C Blues scales. After the solo, the melody returns to finish the piece. Listen to the audio a few times before you dive in.

Example 3f

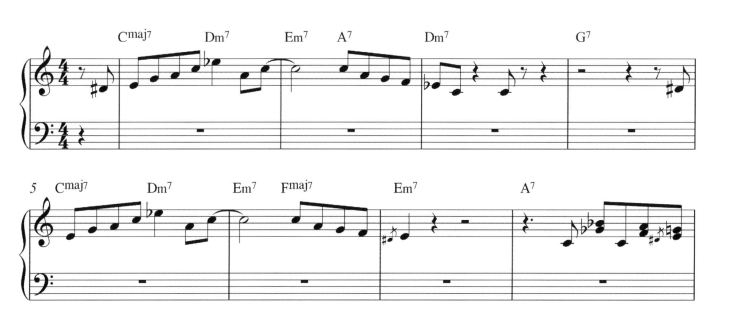

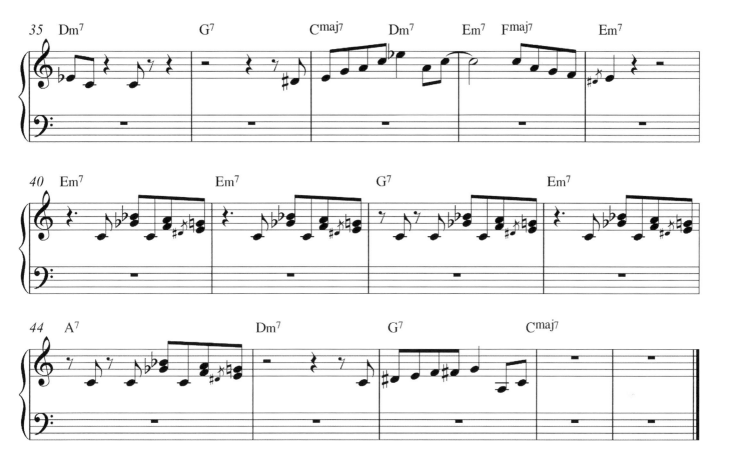

Once you've learned the melody, play along to the Chapter Three backing track. Mix and match the licks you've learned in this chapter to create different ideas every time you come to the solo part. Try to get spontaneous and create your own lines that are inspired by mine.

In the next chapter, we're going to have a change of pace and emphasis.

Chapter Four – Give Me Some Space!

I've often found that as soon as jazz students start to understand which notes to use and gain a bit of confidence, they begin to play lines made up of continuous notes in their solos and don't leave any gaps. Can you imagine if this book was presented with no punctuation or gaps between words?

Itwouldbeprettyhardtofollowafterawhile!

This is what it's like to listen to someone who plays continuously with no gaps. Pretty soon the audience is crying out, "Give us some space, we can't make sense of all these notes!"

In jazz, what you leave out is as important as what you put in, so in this chapter I'm going to give you some exercises and ideas to help you add meaningful space into your playing. Spend some time listening to Count Basie (with his trio or quartet), Ahmed Jamal, Miles Davis and Keith Jarrett. These four jazz legends are all known for their great use of space.

Five exercises to create space in your playing

The first two exercises are designed to be played over the Chapter Four 12-bar Blues in C backing track.

Exercise One

First of all, listen to my playing in Example 4a. What do you notice? I've restricted myself to just four notes and jammed with them exclusively. When you restrict the number of notes you allow yourself to play, it forces you to focus much more on rhythm and placement. It also forces you to get much more creative.

When you play this, please do it for a *long* time. Focus on placing your four notes differently each time. Learn to listen to, appreciate, and enjoy the space that you leave and hear how it punctuates your phrases when you do actually play. Another way to think of this is that the phrases actually serve to punctuate the silence.

Imagine a person who constantly speaks about themselves all the time. We all know one! Now imagine the person who is quiet, but when they do open their mouth, they always say something meaningful and profound. Who do you want to be?

Be self-aware and listen to yourself as you play, as if you were listening to a recording. Also, actually record your playing and, after leaving a good amount of time so you can be objective, listen back and assess your efforts.

Example 4a

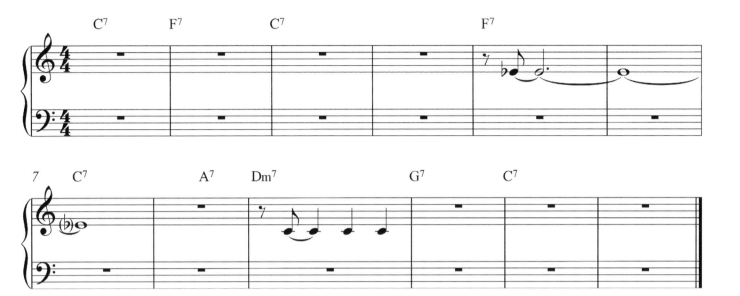

Exercise Two

In this exercise I want you to play another C blues solo. This time the challenge is to play *only one note* from the C blues scale and stick to it throughout the entire solo. You can repeat your chosen note as many times as you like, but the idea is to create something interesting by using rhythm and space. Listen to the solo I've recorded for the example below, then solo yourself with the C blues backing track. Play this for as long as possible every day to force yourself to think in new and creative rhythmic ways.

Example 4b

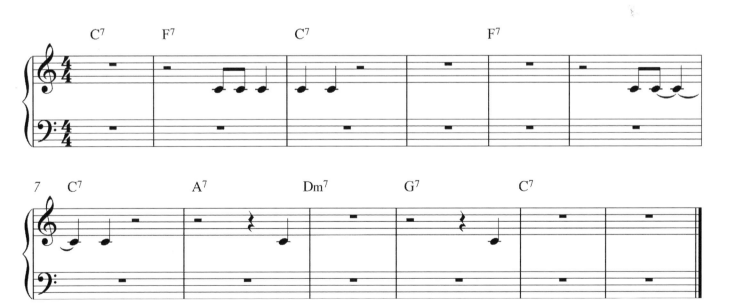

Exercise Three

Before you embark on this next exercise, I want you to listen to the original version of *So What* from Miles Davis' album *Kind of Blue*. Listen especially to Miles' trumpet solo (taking note of his wonderful use of space) and the piano solo near the end of the track by Bill Evans. Evans uses clusters of notes to create colourful chord textures.

In this exercise I want you to do something similar to Bill Evans. This time we'll be using the D Dorian scale. Don't panic if you don't know what that is! All you need to know is that you can use any white note, or any combination of white notes, on the piano.

Listen to and learn my solo first, then play along with the provided Chapter Four D Dorian backing track before trying out your own ideas. I want you to experiment by playing clusters of white notes (any combination will work). Because you don't have to worry about playing the "correct" notes, you can concentrate on your use of space and rhythm.

Example 4c

Exercise Four

For the next exercise we return to the C blues chord progression. I want you to take four of your favourite C blues scale/major pentatonic licks and condense them down. Choose what you consider to be the most important two, three or four notes from each lick. Think about what notes or note combinations give the lick its character and focus on those. By doing this, you are learning to judge what notes are necessary to convey your idea – a crucial facility to have when playing sparsely. Learning to break down your licks is an essential skill that enables you to combine and merge them to form new ideas.

When you have done this, I want you to use the smaller lick fragments (remembering to leave lots of space) to create an engaging solo. Listen to the example I've recorded using fragments from licks 3b and 3c. When you take a few good notes and play them assertively in acres of space it is very effective and interesting.

Example 4d

Exercise Five

In this exercise we'll be taking the previous concept a step further.

The idea is to play a C blues solo with the backing track. However, the rule is to start by playing just the first two notes from one of your licks, leave a good amount of space, then play the first three notes of the same lick, leave some more space, then play the first four notes, adding a note each time you play it.

This approach gives the effect of a small idea developing into something more complex. Try it with some different licks because some will work better than others.

Next repeat the process but without playing a lick as the basis. Simply take two notes that you like, leave some space, then play them again and add one more note each time after leaving some space.

Example 4e uses lick 3a as its inspiration.

Example 4e

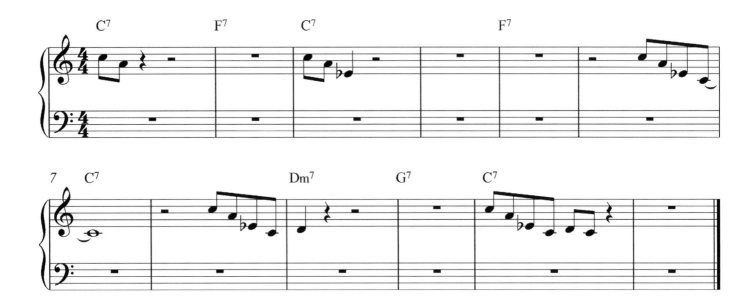

Leaving space in your solos allows time to reflect on the melody you're creating – for both you and your listeners. It creates an atmosphere of expectation and keeps your audience engaged as they wonder what will happen next. It also gives you time to *hear* your next idea in your head and to consider your options before you play it. You have all the time in the world because using space sounds great and really sets you apart as a player.

Use the backing tracks from this chapter to practice soloing, leaving lots of space. Avoid using licks, instead use isolated notes or short phrases here and there to build up some simple, spontaneous ideas.

Chapter Five – The C Minor Pentatonic Scale

The minor pentatonic scale is used extensively in many different styles of music. It is comfortable to play on the guitar and has a powerful, authoritative sound, so it has become a mainstay of Rock, Jazz and Blues. However, if you use it too much, your playing can become reminiscent of a rock guitar solo.

The C minor pentatonic scale is almost identical to the C Blues scale. The only difference is that the C Minor Pentatonic scale doesn't contain a F#. So, if it's so similar to the blues scale, why bother to include it? Well, in jazz, the minor pentatonic can be used in various creative ways that are different to the blues scale and this is what we'll cover in this chapter.

Though pentatonic scales have always been used in jazz piano, they became a big part of the modern jazz piano repertoire through the music of McCoy Tyner. Tyner used combinations of pentatonic scales, mixing and matching them to create powerful, engaging melodic patterns in his solos. We're going to use the C Minor Pentatonic scale to make some McCoy-esque licks.

Make sure you spend some time listening to McCoy Tyner. A good album to start with is *The Real McCoy*. Be sure to check out his piano solo on the track *Passion Dance*.

The C Minor Pentatonic scale contains the notes, C, Eb, F, G and Bb.

Example 5a

Pentatonic scales contain no half step intervals, which is quite a departure from much of the modern jazz vocabulary that uses extensive chromaticism. Knowing how to use pentatonics musically offers you a way to vary the sound of your solo, in the same way you might change your vocabulary to sound more relaxed urgent, friendlier, or formal.

You can vary the character of your jazz vocabulary by playing more chromatic notes, or more pentatonic phrases, or more blues ideas, etc.

C Minor Pentatonic licks

In our opening lick, the interval between the first two notes (C and F) is a fourth. This would be an unusual first step to use in more traditional jazz but is quite common in McCoy Tyner's melodic language and forms part of his unique sound. Keep this in mind when you're composing your own pentatonic licks later. Notice that this idea doesn't end on an obvious resolution note.

Example 5b

The second idea doesn't land on an obvious ending note either. When using pentatonics in this way, choosing more unexpected notes makes the phrase sound as though it's slightly detached from the harmony. This independence from harmonic norms gives us the freedom to experiment with melodic patterns without having to worry so much about what note we're going to resolve to, or which notes are contained in the chord. As long as your melody notes belongs to the minor pentatonic it'll work as a resolution to your phrase.

Example 5c

The next idea is a good example of using stacks of 4ths in our melody to create patterns. For example, F, Bb and Eb are all a fourth apart. This idea is followed by G, C and F, again all a fourth apart.

These large intervals can create an unusual, powerful, dynamic sound that radically transforms the character of your melodic language. For example, when you're playing over a blues, try these ideas after you've been using mostly blues scale vocabulary to create some melodic contrast.

Example 5d

McCoy Tyner often played melodic patterns that repeated in a descending or ascending sequence. Here, we have a simple four-note descending idea starting on Bb, which is then repeated but starting on the next note down in the scale (G), then repeated again a note lower, and so on. This is a simple concept but surprisingly effective and quite easy to do with pentatonics.

Example 5e

For our last example I've decided to create a longer lick to show how some of the concepts above might be combined into a more complete melodic line. See if you can spot some use of 4ths and a short melodic sequence pattern. Listen to its powerful character and play it with a confident touch.

Example 5f

Compose your own licks

Now get creative and compose your own minor pentatonic licks. Focus on using 4ths, melodic patterns in sequences, and don't be too fussy about how the lick ends. Continue to revisit the licks you've written in previous chapters in order to consolidate your vocabulary.

When you've composed a lick, play it multiple times with the Chapter Five Pentatonic backing track. If you get lots of ideas, there's some blank manuscript included in your audio download!

Lick 1

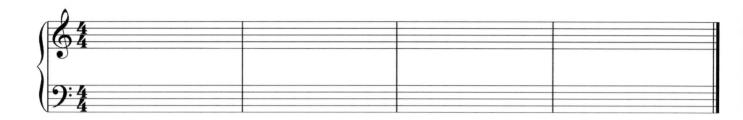

Lick 2

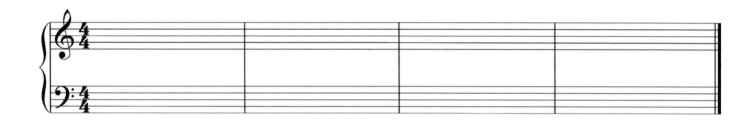

Lick 3

Lick 4

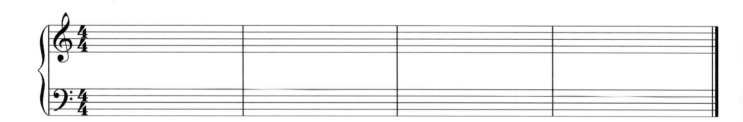

It's time to learn another tune!

This one is written in the style of McCoy Tyner, so now would be a good time to check out his music if you haven't already.

Once again, we're not adding any left-hand notes at this stage, but I've included the chord symbols for when you revisit this tune later on.

Listen to the audio recording of this piece. The melody section is played as written, then there's a solo using only the notes of the C Minor Pentatonic scale. After the solo, the melody returns to finish the piece.

Example 5g

Once you have learned the melody, play along with the backing track. Mix and match the licks you've learned in this chapter to create different ideas every time you come to the solo part. When you get more confident, see if you can invent some spontaneous ideas too.

In the next chapter, we're finally going to look at what you should be doing with your left hand! Later you can come back the tunes in these earlier chapters and add the chords to make the pieces come alive.

Chapter Six – The Left Hand (Part One)

What we do with the left hand is an interesting subject for the jazz pianist. As you may have gathered, a lot of time and effort is put into developing melodic language for the right hand. We treat it like a saxophone or trumpet – a melodic instrument in its own right – and this is a good approach at the start of our journey. Building a fluent stream of melodic ideas that flow through the right hand to create convincing solos is obviously an important goal.

However, as pianists we have a world of opportunity and potential in the left hand. The left hand can play many roles including accompanying the melody, adding a counter melody, combining with the right hand to create textures other instrumentalists can only dream of, through to playing simple chords and basslines.

In this chapter we're going to explore how to accompany ourselves with chords, as this is the main role that falls to the left hand. There are two skills we must develop – each for different musical situations.

Solo piano

The jazz pianist will often be called upon to do solo gigs. This can be a challenging juggling act, as the melody, harmony, bassline and groove all need to be created by you. For the classical pianist there's a huge repertoire of music written for solo piano, but for the jazz musician it's all about combining a diverse set of skills in a creative way.

One of these skills is to be able to read a *lead sheet* (music with just a melody and chord symbols) and improvise a piano arrangement in real time. (The skills required to become a truly proficient solo jazz pianist will be covered in more detail in future books).

With a rhythm section

Playing in a jazz ensemble is one of the most important and pleasurable elements of being a jazz pianist, and it's important to develop the skills for this situation. As pianists we need to be aware of our role and the role of other members of the rhythm section.

The bass player provides the harmonic foundation and rhythmic impetus for the band. The drummer adds to the rhythmic potency and provides not only groove but textures and fills.

The pianist has the job of adding chords to the harmonic foundation laid down by the bass, building up an improvised accompaniment by commenting on and punctuating proceedings with chord stabs, melodic fragments and the many other textures and colours available to the instrument. We call this role *comping* – a shortening of the word *accompanying*.

When it's our turn to solo, the jazz pianist will continue to comp chords and rhythms for himself/herself with the left hand, but before we work on developing this skill, we need to make sure that we understand how jazz chords work and are notated. Let's take a look at the essential chord types.

Basic chords reminder

Major chords

Example 6a illustrates a C Major chord, built from the notes C (root), E (3rd) and G (5th). It's called a major chord because the distance from the root to the 3rd (C to E) is a major 3rd.

Example 6a

Minor chords

For a minor chord, the 3rd is lowered a half step, so we get C (root), Eb (b3) and G (5th). It's called a minor chord because the distance between the C and Eb notes is a minor 3rd. All minor chords have this root –minor 3rd relationship.

Example 6b

The three most used 7th chords

The major and minor chords above were formed with just three notes, called a *triad*. In jazz we almost always play *7th chords* (constructed using four notes), so knowing how to play the three most commonly used 7th chords is essential.

A 7th chord is created by stacking one more 3rd on top of the major or minor triad. The most common types of 7th chord are the major 7th, minor 7th and dominant 7th.

Major 7th chords

Major 7th chords consist of a major triad with a *major 3rd* stacked on top. This can be seen in the following example showing how C Major 7 is built.

Example 6c

Major 7th chords can be written on chord charts in several different ways. For example, a C Major 7th chord may be written as CMaj7, CM7 (notice the uppercase "M" for Major) or C with a small triangle symbol next to it.

Minor 7th chords

Minor 7th chords consist of a minor triad with a *minor 3rd* stacked on top. Here's how C minor 7 is built.

Example 6d

Like major 7th chords, minor 7th chords are written in several different ways on chord charts. C minor 7th may be written as Cmin7, Cm7 (notice the lowercase "m" for minor) or C-7.

Dominant 7th chords

Dominant 7th chords consist of a major triad with a *minor 3rd* added on top. Here's how C7 is built.

Example 6e

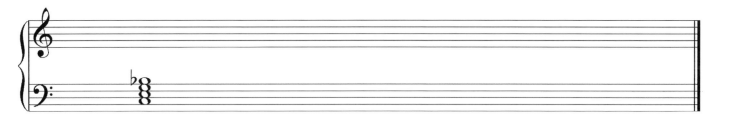

Dominant 7th chords are always written the same way on chord charts. For example, C Dominant 7 will always be written as C7.

Chord finding exercise

Now I want you to create some 7th chords on the piano. I'm going to give you nine chords to find, three of each type of 7th.

Remember the formula for each type of 7th chord:

Maj7 = Major triad with a major 3rd added on top.

Min7 = Minor triad with a minor 3rd added on top.

Dominant 7 = Major triad with a minor 3rd added on top.

See if you can build the chords of:

FMaj7, GMaj7 and BbMaj7.

Then,

Am7, Em7 and Gm7.

Then,

F7, D7 and Bb7.

How did you do? The example below shows the answers.

Listen to the sound of each chord type. You should learn to recognise these flavours by ear as soon as possible. What kind of emotions or images come to mind for each of the chord types: major 7, minor 7 and dominant 7?

Example 6f

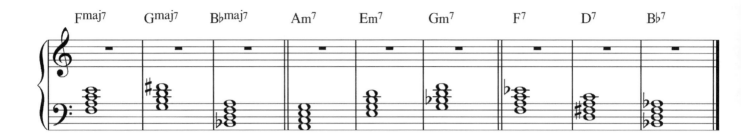

Basic voicings

When we talk about how to *voice* a chord, we're referring to how we choose to distribute the notes of the chord on the keyboard. Chords don't have to be voiced in order i.e. the root note first, then the 3rd, then the 5th, then the 7th. In fact, different configurations or *voicings* of those notes create their own unique sound.

We're going to learn some great all-purpose voicings to get you going, including one where the notes have been reordered. Here are basic voicings for the chords Dm7, G7 and CMaj7.

Example 6g

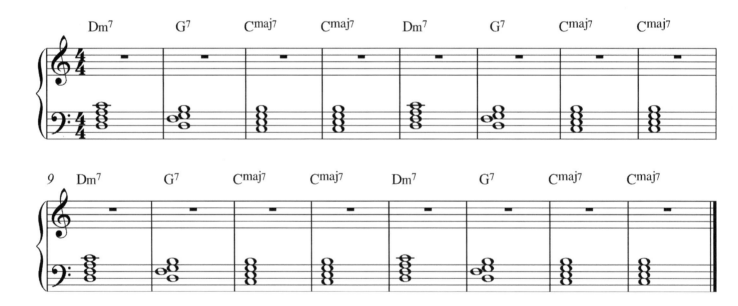

Notice that the G7 chord does not have G as its bass note, but D instead. G7 has the notes G, B, D, F. Here, I've chosen to reorder those notes, placing the D in the bass. This is known as an *inversion*.

Why did I choose to play an inversion here, but play the other chords normally? The answer is simple economy of movement. If I'm busy soloing with the right hand, I want my left hand to play chord voicings that are as convenient as possible. You'll see in the chapters that follow, that 90% of the time in jazz the chord G7 is preceded by the chord Dm7. By placing the D of G7 in the bass, I can keep the root of the Dm7 chord where it is to create a much smoother chord change.

Take some time to get used to these voicings. Practice them until you can play them without looking down at your left hand. In Example 6g, all the chords are played on beat 1 and last the full duration of the bar. This is an acceptable way to play but, of course, will quickly become very boring! So, in the next chapter we're going to use these voicings to explore the rhythmic side of comping.

Chapter Seven – The Left Hand (Part Two)

Adding syncopation

As a jazz pianist, we have a great deal of freedom in what we choose to play when we accompany ourselves. Comping is quite an individual thing and every master of jazz piano has their own approach to left hand accompaniment. Thelonious Monk's left hand sounds very different to Bill Evans' and Evans sounds very different to McCoy Tyner, and so on. This has something to do with the chord voicings each chooses to play, but is also determined by their rhythmic approach and by how much/how little they play.

First, here are two general principles to keep in mind when thinking about the role of the left hand:

1. For the majority of the time, the left hand's role is accompaniment, so it should play more softly than the right hand, which will generally be soloing.

2. It's always tempting to play too much in the left hand, but the axiom *less is more* is especially true here. You don't have to play every chord. If you have a bass player covering the root notes, you don't need to fill in 100% of the harmony – the listener will still be able to understand what's going on.

With that said, let's look at how we can make the basic voicings we learned in the previous chapter sound more interesting by adding some *syncopation*.

This basically means off beat rhythms, but even if you're not familiar with the word, you'll be familiar with the sound of a syncopated rhythm. Example 7a shows the opening phrase of a nursery rhyme. The first time through it is written as we would normally sing it. The second time through, it's written with syncopation added to the last two notes. They now land on the second half of beat one and the second half of beat two, off the main beat. You can hear the difference and you might even say that it sounds jazzier.

Example 7a

All jazz pianists use syncopated rhythms as part of their style, so to help you get comfortable with syncopated chords we'll work through some exercises.

In Example 7b every chord is placed on the second half of beat one. Listen to the audio example and play along with it if you find this tough.

Example 7b

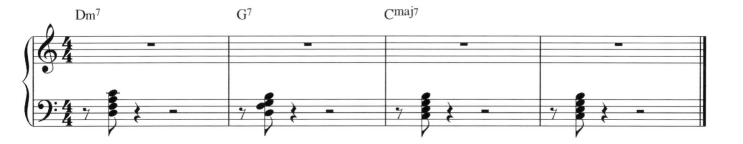

This time, we'll place each chord on the second half of beat two.

Example 7c

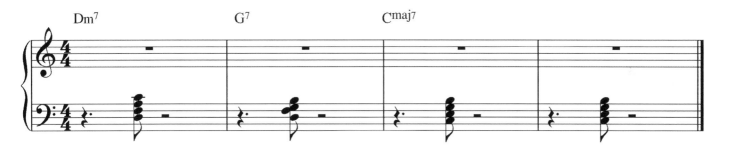

Now on the second half of beat three.

Example 7d

Notice what a difference these simple syncopations make to how the left hand accompaniment sounds.

Moving the emphasis to the second half of beat four is a technique many jazz pianists use to anticipate the chord that will follow. For instance, we might play a G7 chord at the end of a bar marked Dm7 in order to anticipate the G7 in the next bar. Pay attention though, the anticipation means that this example starts on the second half of beat four in the count-in!

Example 7e

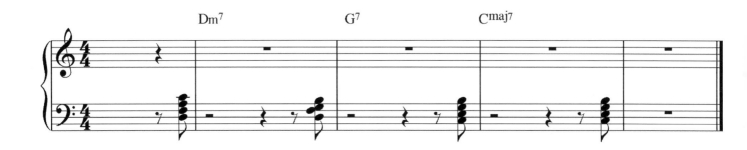

The dotted 1/4 and 1/8th note combination is a rhythm that comes up again and again when you listen to jazz pianists comping. Listen to Example 7f to hear how this sounds. Let's use a similar process to the one we've just used to practice this, first starting on beat one.

Example 7f

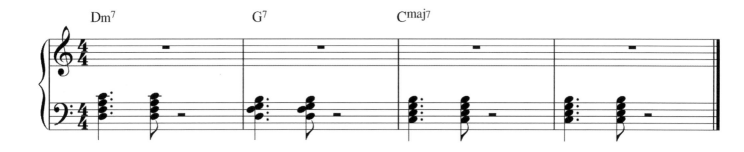

Now on beat two.

Example 7g

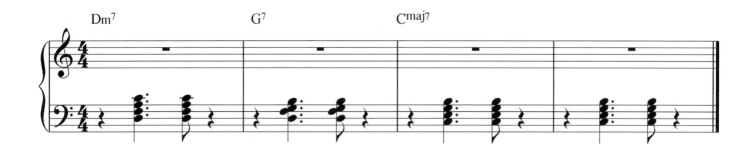

In the next example, the 1/8th notes land on the second half of beat 4. So, as in Example 7e, we anticipate the chord in the next bar.

Example 7h

Here are some more rhythm ideas for comping. Try playing them on beat 1, then 2, then 3. If you can, try them on beat 4 as well.

Example 7i

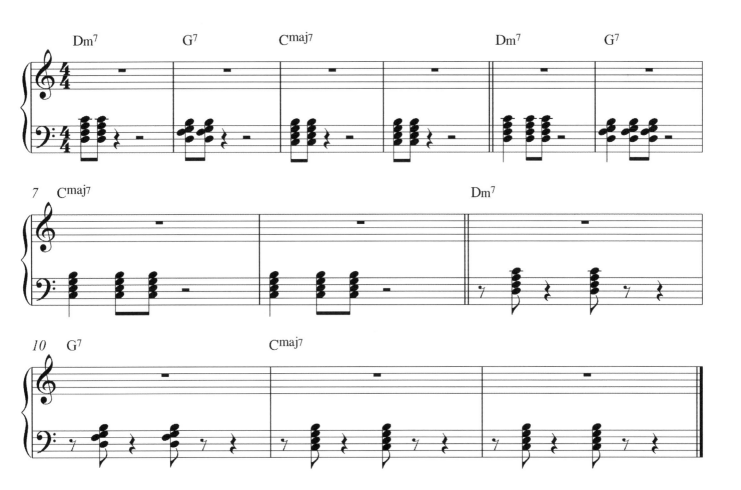

In the next two examples you can see how one might comp with some of the licks you learned earlier. These are based on the licks from examples 3d and 3e. You should also spot some of the rhythms we've just practiced.

Example 7j

Here is a good example of "less is more" comping, using just a few 1/8th note stabs.

Example 7k

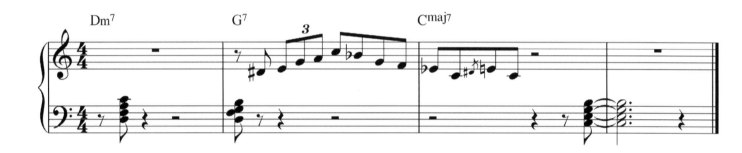

To end this chapter, here are two exercises to help you put into practice what you've learned.

Exercise 1:

Using the chord voicings we've learned for Dm7, G7 and CMaj7, play the chords written in Example 7l along with the Chapter Seven backing track provided.

Use only your left hand and explore some of the rhythms we've practiced. See if you can get to the point where you can play the chords with your eyes shut. Being able to play these left hand voicings automatically is important – you are working towards being able to solo fluently with your right hand and add left hand chords without thinking.

Example 71

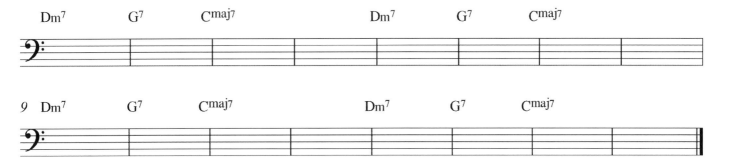

Exercise 2:

Once you are comfortable playing the left hand chords, try some simple right hand soloing ideas. Use some of your licks from the first three chapters. When you're more confident, try some spontaneous ideas using the C Major Pentatonic and C Blues scales.

A good approach is to play a lick in the right hand, then leave some space to add one or two left hand chord stabs. Then play another right hand idea and do the same again. This is a great way to begin to practice comping for yourself.

Meanwhile, listen lots to your favourite jazz pianists and notice what they're doing with their left hand when they're playing with a rhythm section.

Chapter Eight – Playing the Changes (Part One)

Jazz pianists *love* chords and what we can do with them, and much of what gives jazz soloing its distinctive sound is the manipulation of harmony, and what we choose to play over a given chord.

When it comes to soloing, there's no way around it: if we want an authentic jazz vocabulary, we can't just play pentatonics all the time – we have to navigate our solos with a strong awareness of the underlying harmony. In practice, this means playing something that interlocks with the notes in the chord changes. Jazz musicians call this *playing the changes*. This can be challenging, but it's what creates melodic sounds that no doubt first attracted you to jazz music.

To begin the process of soloing *with* the chord changes (as opposed to playing one scale *over* the changes), we're going to use the most common chord coupling in all styles of Western music: the perfect cadence. But first, I want to quickly explain how jazz musicians refer to the different chords in a key.

As you probably know, we can build a chord on every note of a scale. For example, using the scale of C Major, we can build the chords C Major, D minor, E minor, F Major, G Major, A minor and B minor flat 5.

Notice that some chord *qualities* are major and some are minor. When you build chords on the Major scale, the order of chord qualities always follows the same pattern:

Major, Minor, Minor, Major, Major, Minor, Minor b5.

Because these chord qualities appear in the same order in every major key, we can use a shorthand system to refer to them that works in *every* key. In shorthand, each chord is assigned a Roman number, so that we have chord I, chord II, etc. The table below shows the chords in the key of C Major with Roman numerals below. (Roman numerals are still pronounced like the numbers they represent, so V is pronounced "five").

Chord	C Major	D minor	E minor	F Major	G Major	A minor	B minor b5
Roman numeral	I	II	III	IV	V	VI	VII

Using the shorthand system, chord I in the key of C is C Major; chord II is D minor; chord V is G Major, etc.

This system is incredibly useful for jazz musicians, who use it to quickly communicate a chord sequence that works in any key. For example, we might say something like, "Play a II V I in the key of C." That would mean, play the chords D minor, G Major, then C Major.

What if we wanted to play a II V I in the key of G?

Remembering that all major keys follow the same pattern of chord qualities, we can quickly work out that we'd play A minor, D Major, then G Major.

Can you figure out what the II V I chords are in the keys of F Major and D Major?

You'll hear jazz musicians talk about sequences of chords as units like this all the time. They might say something like, "Do you know any good II V I licks?" or "This tune is based around a I VI II V sequence in Bb Major" etc.

Now you have a grounding in shorthand chord notation, let's move on to look at soloing over the most important chord sequence in jazz – the V I. If you're from a classical background, you'll recognise this as the *perfect cadence*.

You know now that in the key of C Major, the V chord is G Major and the I chord is C Major. However, as we're jazz musicians, we want to play this cadence with 7th chords, so we'll stack another 3rd onto each chord as before and play G7 to CMaj7.

The V I perfect cadence is so significant because it is the chord movement that occurs in pretty much all pieces of music. It sounds like a musical "full stop". The V chord sets up an expectation; it sounds like it needs to resolve to the I chord. When it does, it feels like we've arrived home. You'll probably recognise this next little fragment of music that illustrates the perfect cadence beautifully.

Play this short example, but stop before the C chord at the end and don't play the last chord. The excerpt will sound incomplete and you'll probably feel a strong urge to play the last chord. This is because of the V chord's strong gravitational pull towards chord I. Welcome to the world of the perfect cadence, the law of musical gravity.

Now play Example 8a again, but this time resolve to the I chord at the end.

Example 8a

V I chord licks

Now it's time to begin developing some jazz vocabulary over this important cadence. Here are five licks you need to know that *outline* chords of G7 to CMaj7. In other words, they strongly spell out the harmony.

To begin with, our aim is to *articulate* each underlying chord in our solos. The best way to begin doing this is to play a note from the new chord when a chord change occurs.

In my melody over the G7, I'll play the notes in that chord (G, B, D and F), and when the chord changes to CMaj7, I'll play the notes in that chord (C, E, G and B).

This is a great exercise to learn to play the chord changes. You're not going to create any ground-breaking music just yet, but later, when you combine this approach with the scale-based approach of chapters 1-5, you'll hear how articulate your playing immediately becomes. For now, however, we need to train ourselves to become adept at outlining the changes and get those shapes in our heads.

Example 8b starts by outlining the notes of the G7 chord clearly in bar one.

On the first beat of bar two, we land on the E of the CMaj7 chord. Notice that this note isn't in the chord of G7, but *is* in the chord of CMaj7. This makes it a great note to point to the new chord. The note E is the major 3rd of the CMaj7 chord. The 3rd of any chord is a great note to aim for, to articulate the chord change clearly in your solo.

Example 8b

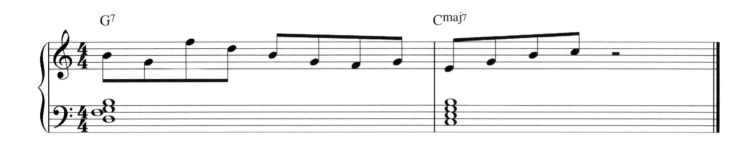

I wanted to make Example 8c sound as tuneful as possible while still only using the tones of the chords. One way of doing this is to use fewer notes. In bar one I imply the G7 chord by picking out the root (G) and the 5th (D) and climbing to the root again. If you omit the 3rd of a chord, it has the effect of suggesting the chord without being too descriptive (because 3rds and 7ths are the notes that most describe the chord *quality*).

You may notice that I've "cheated" a little in my final note choice of bar one by playing an early E in anticipation of the CMaj7 in bar two. Anticipating a chord change by playing a note that belongs to the next chord *before* it arrives is a well-established strategy that gives your solos a sense of forward momentum. To do this well, you need to be keenly aware of the notes in the coming chord.

Example 8c

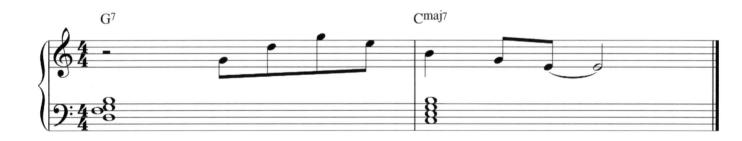

In the next example, I am much more specific in my note choice, clearly spelling out G7 from top to bottom. The final F note of bar one resolves to the E at the beginning of bar two.

In bar two I run up the notes of the CMaj7 chord but leave out the root. Omitting the obvious sounding root note can give the lick a slightly "removed from the chord" sound without sounding dissonant. This is a good trick to use when you write your own licks.

Example 8d

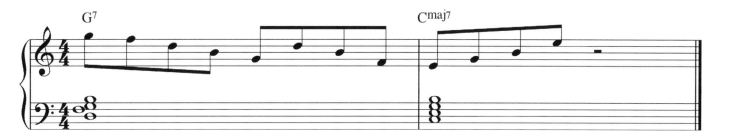

For Example 8e, although this is just an exercise (and most of the licks in this section will sound a bit mechanical), I've tried to make it sound melodic. Learning to make just the basic arpeggio notes sound as tuneful as possible is a useful creative exercise to work on.

Notice that I don't use all the chord tones. In bar two, I only use E and B over the CMaj7 chord, finishing my lick on the 7th (B) of the I chord. Finishing on the 7th like this can give the lick the "removed" sound mentioned earlier

Example 8e

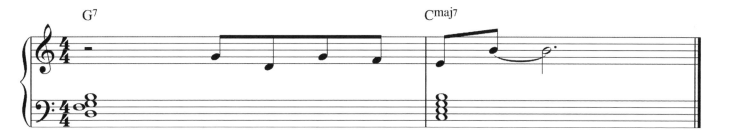

In this final lick I take advantage of the notes G7 and CMaj7 have in common. In the first bar, I play the notes of a G Major triad (G, B, D). To make this idea fit over the CMaj7 chord, I simply change the note D to E. It is useful to explore the common notes shared by chords when soloing, as they can be a safe option in the heat of the moment.

Example 8f

Compose Your Own Licks

Now it's time for you to create your own licks over the V to I chord progression.

Remember that the point of this chapter has been to limit ourselves to chord tones, to strongly spell the underlying harmony and highlight the difference between the chords. Don't be discouraged if the licks you invent sound a bit mechanical – you're just learning to navigate the changes. Once you're really familiar with the notes, you can focus more on rhythm to make your lines as interesting as possible.

When you've composed a lick, play it multiple times with the provided Chapter Eight backing track. I've recorded bass and drums this time, but no piano chords. When you feel confident playing your lick with the right hand, see if you can add the left-hand chord voicings for G7 and CMaj7 that we learned in the previous chapter.

Lick 1

Lick 2

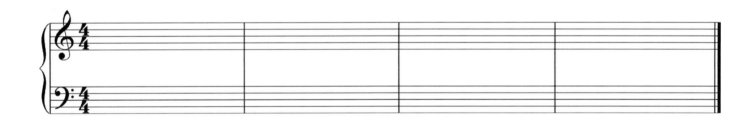

Lick 3

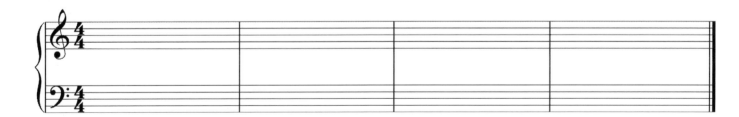

Lick 4

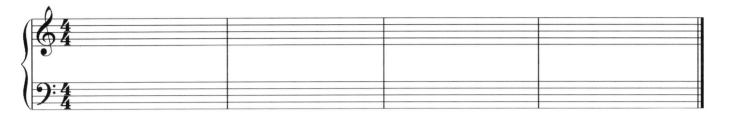

Finally, it's time to learn another tune. The melody only uses chord tones and I've added the basic left hand chord voicings from the previous chapter. The melody section is played as written, then there's a solo using only the notes belonging to the chords. After the solo, the melody returns to finish the piece.

Example 8g

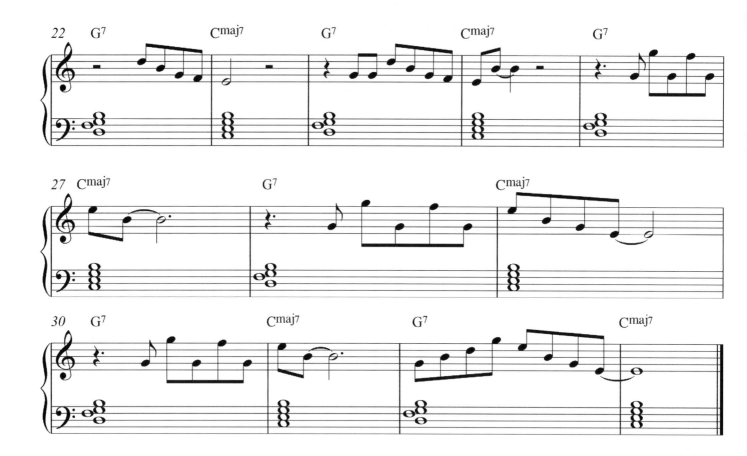

Once you've learned the melody thoroughly, and have played through the example, play along with the backing track and experiment. Mix and match the lines you've learned in this chapter to create different ideas every time you come to the solo part. When you get more confident, see if you can invent some spontaneous ideas too.

In the next chapter, we're going to take what we've learned about soloing over the V to I chord sequence a step further.

Chapter Nine – Playing the Changes (Part Two)

In this chapter we will build on our work with the perfect cadence in Chapter Eight and start exploring the chord sequence that every jazz musician knows best: the II V I.

In the key of C Major, this chord sequence comprises the chords Dmin7 (II), G7 (V) and CMaj7 (I).

In the previous chapter we discussed the *gravitational pull* of the V chord towards the I chord. This pull is also present when moving from chord II to chord V, because the root notes are also a perfect fifth interval apart.

In less jazzy music, chord IV (F) is often played before chord V (G), but jazz musicians favour the sound of the 5th interval movement. In the following example, you'll hear that the Dmin7 sounds warmer and fuller than the plain F chord.

Example 9a

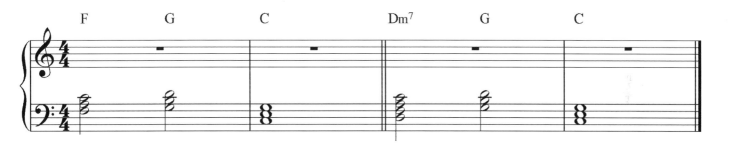

The II V I chord sequence is used extensively in jazz standards and you'll find yourself having to solo over this progression in all keys and at all sorts of speeds. When you are a fluent improviser over the II V I sequence, you'll have already accomplished a great deal, and you'll be fluent over a huge portion of the jazz repertoire, as it is such an intrinsic part of learning the jazz language.

Let's try out some II V I lines.

II V I licks

Here are five licks written over the chord progression of II V I in C Major. As before, I've restricted myself to chord tones only.

Learn each lick slowly and try singing it while playing to help internalise the sound and chord tone patterns.

I've written in the left hand chord voicings for each bar. However, don't be bound by the written rhythm – feel free to use any of the comping rhythms you learned earlier.

In Example 9b, notice my use of anticipation. The final note of bar one is B, which doesn't belong to the chord of Dm7 but does belong to G7. This B gives the G7 much of its gravitational character and is therefore a strong melody note. To throw it in before the G7 chord has officially arrived jolts the ear forward into the next bar early and gives an exciting feeling of forward momentum. The final note of bar two is a B again, which also belongs to CMaj7 and subtly anticipates the next bar.

Example 9b

Example 9c continues the triplet arpeggio idea used at the end of the previous lick and turns it into the main feature. In a wider context, the idea of taking a feature from a lick you just played and using it as the main feature of the next creates a sense of *narrative* in your solo. Developing an idea creates the feeling of your solo growing, or a plot unfolding, which is exciting for listeners and players alike.

Example 9c

Bar one of Example 9d combines triplets and an anticipated B (features from the first two licks). In bar two, I use notes that work over both the G7 and CMaj7 chords, so I can repeat the same idea in both bars. Playing the same melodic phrase or *motif* in a different harmonic context is a great jazzy trick.

Example 9d

It might be tricky to wrap your fingers around the next example but do your best to learn it.

Here we have a four-bar unbroken melodic line reminiscent of the bebop playing of Charlie Parker or Bud Powell. Both musicians tended to sprinkle their longer melodic lines with an assortment of triplets and 1/16th notes to break up their rhythms. Rhythmic variety is a very important part of any jazz solo.

Example 9e

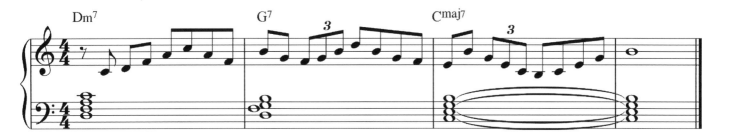

In this final lick, the C note on beat 4 of bar one is the 7th of the Dm7 chord, and is very satisfyingly resolved by landing on the note of B (the 3rd of G7) on the first beat of bar two.

At the end of bar two we use the same device, dropping from F (the 7th of G7) to an E (the 3rd of CMaj7) on beat 1 of bar three.

This idea of playing the 7th of one chord and dropping to the 3rd of the next is a common and pleasing device used extensively by jazz pianists.

Example 9f

As a side note, I hope you can see how important it is to remember these arpeggio shapes. Not only do they help outline each chord, they're also a great way to launch yourself up the keyboard into a higher register.

Now it's time again to create your own licks over the II V I chord progression.

Remember the different strategies you can use, like leaving space, playing triplets, using arpeggios, and anticipating chord changes. Continue to revisit the licks you've written in previous chapters to consolidate your vocabulary.

When you have composed a lick, play it multiple times over the Chapter Nine backing track. I've recorded bass and drums but no piano chords. When you feel confident playing your lick with the right hand, see if you can add the left hand chord voicings for Dm7, G7 and CMaj7 that you learned earlier.

Lick 1

Lick 2

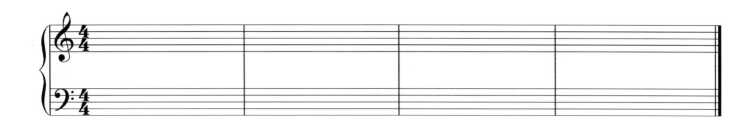

Lick 3

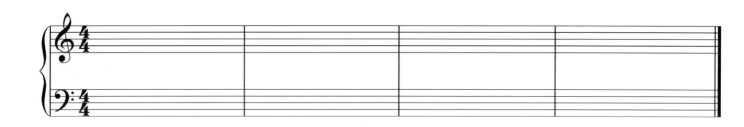

Lick 4

Learn a tune

Here is another tune to learn. The melody uses chord tones and I've written in the basic left hand chord voicings that we learned in Chapter Six. I've written the chords in 1/2 note rhythm but feel free to explore different left hand comping rhythms.

The melody section is played as written, then there's a solo using chord tones. After the solo, the melody returns to finish the piece.

Example 9g

As before, play along to this chapter's backing track and mix and match the licks you've learned to create different ideas each time you come to the solo. When you get more confident, try to invent some spontaneous ideas.

Chapter Ten – Playing the Changes with Passing Notes (Part Three)

In the previous two chapters we began to build our jazz vocabulary by playing over the most common of jazz progressions, using the tones of the underlying chords to form our melodic lines. Now we take things a step further by joining the dots! In other words, connecting the chord tones by adding *passing notes*.

Passing notes are simply notes played to move between one note destination and another. This is illustrated in Example 10a. The notes of a CMaj7 chord are seen as solid black notes, while the light grey notes in between indicate the passing notes that occur between the chord tones.

When we add passing notes in between the CMaj7 chord tones, it gives us all the notes of the C Major scale.

Example 10a

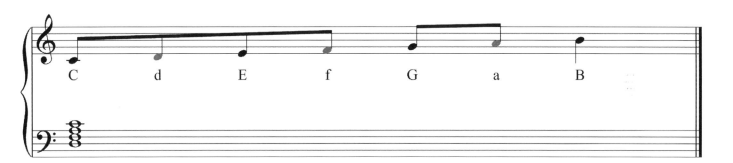

Passing notes help us to make our licks sound more melodic, allowing us to use *any note* in the major scale. However, we mustn't throw away the work we've done in previous chapters – we still need to keep the chord tones in mind when we solo. An awareness of the chord tones gives us a strong framework for our solo, and we can use it to move from chord tone to chord tone, playing occasional passing notes to add more interest.

We'll begin exploring this idea with some simple exercises, using the II V I progression in C Major. For now, I've marked the passing notes with a * so they immediately jump out at you. The three exercises that follow will get you used to inserting passing notes into arpeggios.

As well as getting your fingers used to the shapes of these exercises, get your ears used to the different character the passing notes bring.

Example 10b

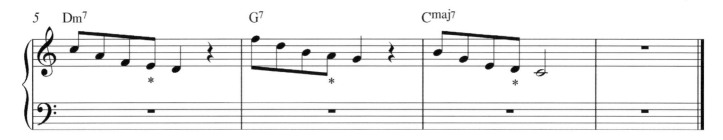

Example 10c

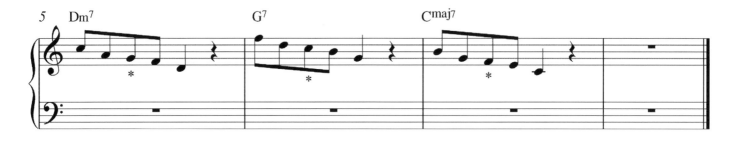

Example 10d

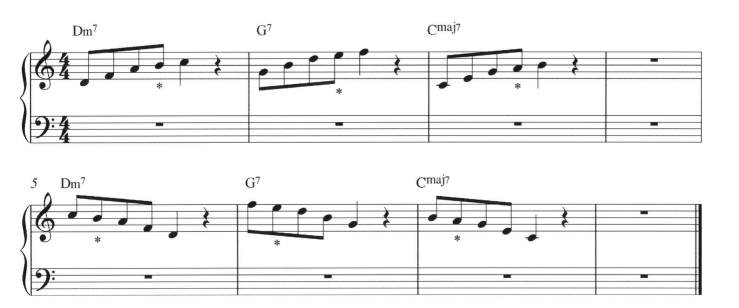

Six licks using passing notes

Now here are six passing note licks for you to learn. As before, do your best to commit them to memory, so that they become a part of your musical vocabulary. The passing notes are marked with an * as before. Basic left hand chords are indicated, but use any of the rhythms you've learned to play them.

In examples 10e and 10f, listen to how the addition of just three or four passing notes gives the lick a much more melodic sound. These lines don't sound mechanical any more, but elegantly express the chords.

Example 10e

Example 10f

For Example 10g I have written out the lick twice. The second time, I've faded the off beat notes to highlight the strong chord tone structure of the lick. Notice that a chord tone lands on every beat.

Not every lick has chord tones landing on every beat like this one, but more often than not, chord tones are played on the strong beats in jazz. This approach can give a lick a logical sense of direction, as it moves from one harmonic destination to the next. It's good to keep this in mind when writing your own licks: as a rule of thumb, choose chord tones to land on the strong beats of one and three.

Example 10g

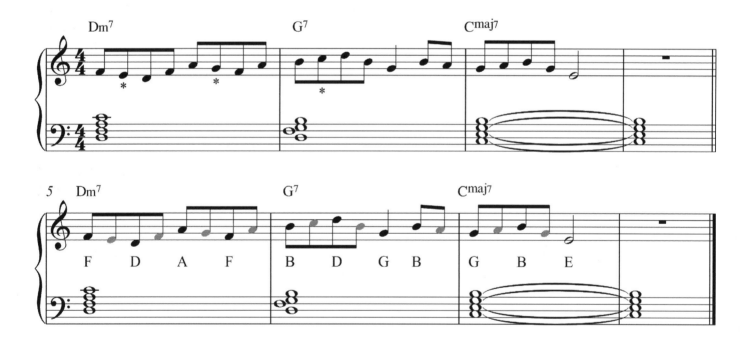

Our last lick of this section is much more scalic than the other licks. We've already seen that when we fill in a seventh chord by playing all the passing notes in between the chord tones, we have a scale! Continue to be mindful of the underlying chord tones as you play. Even if they fit the chords, scales can sound somewhat directionless unless you have a destination note in mind.

Example 10h

A short introduction to chromatic passing notes

Although this is a concept that will be explored in the next book in this series, to end this chapter we'll take a brief look at the idea of *chromatic passing notes*. Using chromatics is one of the signature characteristics of the jazz sound, but is a huge subject! That said, I'll give you a taste of it here and pass on a few handy tricks.

A chromatic passing note is a non-scale tone. We've been playing extensively in the key of C Major, so only using the white keys of the piano. A chromatic scale is a series of notes using every key, black and white. Chromatic runs are used extensively in jazz music but when used inexpertly they can sound directionless and random. Here are two simple, effective tricks using chromatic passing notes.

The first is to add a chromatic passing note between the root and the 7th when descending to the 7th note of a chord. In Example 10i we will use this idea on both the Dm7 and G7 chords. This is an easy but very effective strategy to add that authentic chromatic jazz sound on minor seventh and dominant seventh chords. (NB: this trick does *not* work on major 7 chords as there is only a half step distance between the root and 7th).

Example 10i

The second trick is to add chromatic passing notes between minor thirds. The distance of a minor third is only three half steps, so we can use this idea to create a short but effective chromatic run.

Look for the minor third distances between your chord tones (see Chapter Six for a refresher) and play chromatically from one to the other. In bar one of Example 10j we have a chromatic run between the notes A and C. Bar two's chromatic passing notes are between the minor third of B and D, and in bar three we use E and G. Get used to the rhythmic space this short run takes up and the character of the sound by learning the lick really well.

Example 10j

Now it's time for you to get creative again and write your own licks using chord tones and passing notes. Try using the chromatic tricks in at least one of your licks.

Lick 1

Lick 2

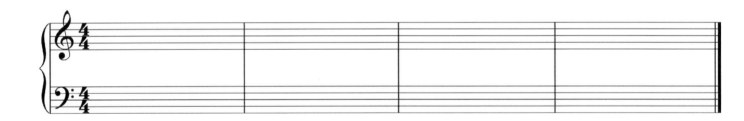

Lick 3

Lick 4

Now move on to Chapter Eleven where we'll bring everything you've learned together.

Chapter Eleven – Bringing It All Together

It's important to consolidate all that we've learned so far. Recap every chapter of the book, using one practice session for each. Replay the licks and the pieces, reflect on the character of the scale or concept in each chapter, and listen to the examples. As you work through the first five chapters, see if you can comp the chords along with the licks and pieces as you play them.

After you have recapped each chapter, complete the following exercises, chapter by chapter. A PDF of some blank manuscript paper comes with the audio download of this book from **www.fundamental-changes.com/ audio-downloads**.

Chapter One

Write a new major pentatonic lick.

Take elements of two licks from Chapter One to create another new lick.

Chapter Two

Write a new blues scale lick.

Combine elements of two licks from Chapter Two to create another new lick.

Chapter Three

Write a new major pentatonic/blues scale lick.

Combine elements of two licks from Chapter Three to create another new lick.

Chapter Four

Write a four-bar blues scale lick using only four notes.

Chapter Five

Write a new C Minor Pentatonic lick that uses 4ths.

Combine elements of two licks from Chapter Five to create another new lick.

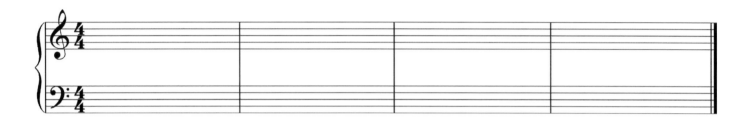

Chapters Six and Seven

Create the chords of EbMaj7, EMaj7, Cmin7, Fmin7, A7 and Eb7 using the formulas.

Here are the answers:

Example 11a

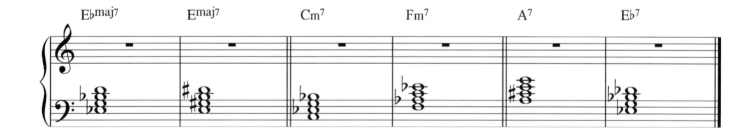

Chapter Eight

Write a new V I chord progression lick.

Combine elements of two licks from Chapter Eight to create another new 'V I' lick.

Chapter Nine

Write a new II V I chord progression lick.

Combine elements of two licks from Chapter Nine to create another new II V I lick.

Chapter Ten

Write a new II V I chord progression lick with passing notes.

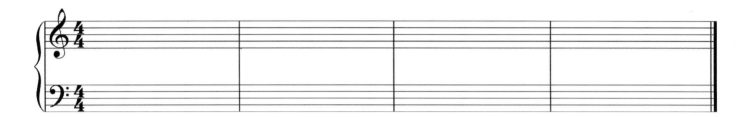

Combine elements of two licks from Chapter Ten to create another new II V I lick.

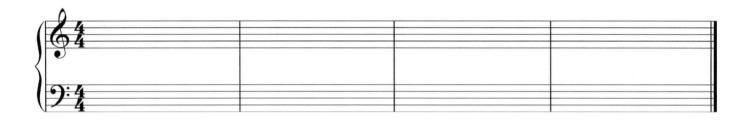

Learn a tune

Now it's time to learn one final tune. Here, I've brought together many of the different elements we've covered in this book. I've also written an analysis of the improvised solo I played, so that you can hear and see some of the concepts working in a longer excerpt.

The melody of this piece runs from bars 1-32 (marked as "Head" at the beginning) and the solo begins in bar 33. I've written 1/2 note left hand chord voicings but please feel free to comp as you see fit. In the solo there are some good licks and tricks for you to wrap your fingers around.

Four things to find in the solo

1. Can you find a bar in the solo that uses only notes from the C Major Pentatonic scale?

2. Can you find a bar in the solo that uses only notes from the C Blues scale? (This one is tough, there's only one bar that uses purely blues scale).

3. Can you find a bar in the solo that uses a mix of the blues scale and the major pentatonic scale?

4. Can you find a II V I lick that uses only chord tones?

Now listen to the audio of Example 11b and try playing through the whole piece. If you find parts of it tricky, stop and focus just on those bars, slowing things right down.

Once you can play the solo, read my analysis of it carefully to help you appreciate all that's going on.

Example 11b

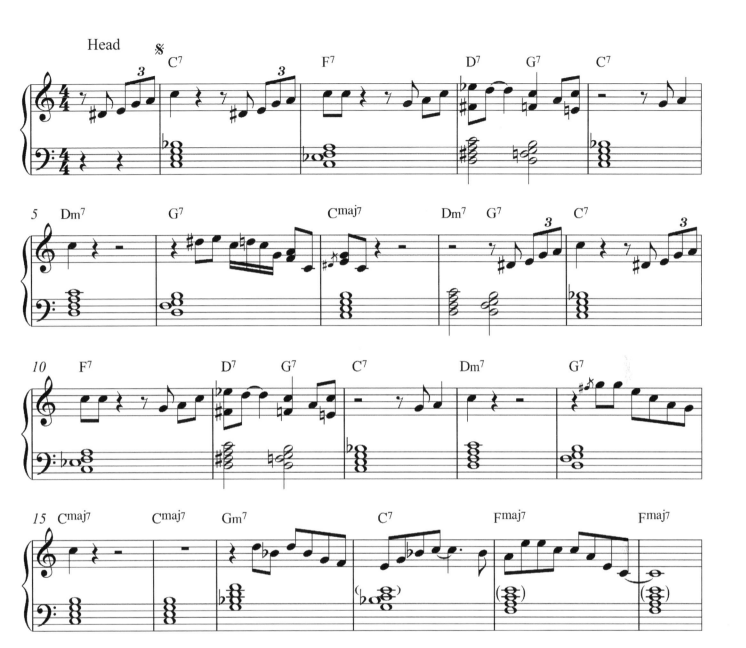

Analysis

The solo begins at the end of bar thirty-two. The first phrase uses mostly notes from the C Major Pentatonic scale, finishing on beat 1 of bar thirty-four. The last two notes of the first phrase are then reiterated and subtly embellished with a grace note before the A, and there's an extra C on the end. Six rest beats follow, allowing some space to breath.

A simple, more bluesy descending figure breaks the silence at the end of bar thirty-six. This descending figure runs down the notes of the C Major Pentatonic scale but replaces the E with an Eb. The effect of this small tweak is quite transformative and creates a bluesy flavour. The descending figure is followed by an ascending phrase which features a chromatic run up from D# to G (which is allowed in our mixture of major pentatonic and blues!)

From bar forty, things start to lift off. The solo still continues to use major pentatonic/blues scale combinations but to add emphasis and excitement we have some octaves, two-note chords and more notes generally. In bar 46 the blues scale note of Bb features three times within the first three beats, but right at the end of the bar the

Bb is raised to a B natural, which belongs to the chord of G7. Here we're mixing blues scale notes and chord tones to create a pleasing lick which gives the line a bluesy character but points satisfyingly to the harmony.

Next, we come to an interesting turn in the harmony in bars 49-52. It is best to think of these chords as a II V I in the key of F Major: Gm7 – C7 – FMaj7. It is a good idea to transpose your licks into different keys. At this stage of your playing it's good to at least know them in the keys of F and G, as well as C. Then it becomes easy to negotiate these brief key changes that are so common in jazz.

From the key change in bar forty-nine the solo becomes much less bluesy and more focused on the chord changes, using chord tones and passing notes through to the end of bar fifty-five. This is to help the listener understand where the harmony is going and to point out the beauty of the chord changes. What's the use of having a lovely harmony if our melodic lines don't reflect it? In bar fifty-three we fixate on the note D. This is a massive anticipation of the D7 chord coming a bar later. Notice how you can bend the rules with these anticipations and use this tactic to play outside the box.

A nice chord tone lick over the II V chords takes us back to C major (chord I) in bars 55-56. Even before we arrive at the I chord, however, we anticipate our return to the home key by plunging back into the blues again. The change of character from chord tones to blues reflects the change of chord type – bars 57-60 consist only of dominant 7th chords, and when you have only dominant 7th chords it makes the harmony sound bluesy. We continue with the tasty blues/major pentatonic licks until bar sixty where we use a Dmin7 arpeggio (in anticipation of the chord in the next bar) to launch ourselves into the upper register of the piano. This exciting move brings us to the climax of the solo, concluding with a descending flurry of bluesy triplets to bring us back to a middle C.

Go beyond the licks

It may take you some time to get the solo up to speed but do persevere because there's much to be gained in knowledge, inspiration and technique by learning solos. Listen to solos by your favourite jazz musicians and seek out transcriptions of the ones you like. It's easy to get hold of solo transcriptions via the Internet these days, or you could try the old-fashioned way of attempting to transcribe it yourself straight from the record.

If this sounds daunting, don't worry. If you've worked diligently through every chapter of this book, you've already written 43 of your own licks and learned 36 of mine! You've achieved more than you probably realise, and the process of learning, writing and reflecting has built up many of the skills you need for jazz piano soloing.

We've used these licks to begin filling your musical phrasebook, but you can't speak a language fluently if all you do is recite phrases. To speak fluently, you need to be able to develop your ideas, express your thoughts and respond to specific situations.

To gain more freedom, mix up your licks and combine them. Use fragments of them and develop them into new spontaneous ideas. Play them in different ways by varying the rhythm, embellishing or altering some of the notes. There is no "proper" way to play a lick. In fact, the only "real" jazz approach is to try and play it differently every time.

Once you understand how a language works and become comfortable speaking it, the phrases become spontaneous speech. You'll have days where you feel inspired and new ideas flow easily, and other days where you find yourself falling back heavily on learned licks. Don't worry, that's normal!

Above all, listen to lots of jazz, as this will help you create (or steal) new ideas. Add them into your playing and soon they will become your own personal language.

Conclusion (Where To Go From Here)

I do hope that you've enjoyed this book and have been able to draw knowledge and inspiration from it. Jazz is a creative art that thrives on spontaneity and though this book has many examples to learn, they are all designed to develop your own fluent musical speech.

Find a friendly jazz jam session where you can go and play with others to exercise your new vocabulary. Playing with other people, listening to their solos, discussing concepts and approaches, is the quickest way to grow as a jazz musician. If you can, play with people who are better than you, because this will accelerate your progress. I remember many times where I couldn't cope with faster tempos or lost my place in chord progressions. These were all great learning experiences!

If you feel frustrated in a practice session, take a break and perhaps have a listen to one of your favourite jazz recordings to remind yourself of why you're on this journey.

In the next book, *Intermediate Jazz Piano Soloing*, we will build on the vocabulary that we have learned here. We will look more deeply into the use of chromatics, build up confidence in other keys, take a look at more complex harmony and start to learn some of the secrets behind the bebop jazz vocabulary.

Enjoy your playing!

Nathan

Made in United States
Orlando, FL
13 January 2022